F+P - M

AR 3.0
0.5

Holiday Histories

Thanksgiving Day

Mir Tamim Ansary

Heinemann Library
Chicago, Illinois

Customer Service 888-454-2279
Visit our website at www.heinemannraintree.com

Designed by Kimberly Miracle and Q2A Creative
Printed in China by South China Printing Company

10 09 08 07 06
10 9 8 7 6 5 4 3 2 1

New edition ISBNs: 1-4034-8892-4 (hardcover)
                            1-4034-8905-X (paperback)

The Library of Congress has cataloged the first edition as follows:
Ansary, Mir Tamim.
      Thanksgiving Day / Mir Tamim Ansary.
          p. cm. -- (Holiday histories)
      Includes bibliographical references and index.
      ISBN 1-58810-224-6 (lib. bdg.)
      1. Thanksgiving Day – Juvenile literature. [1. Thanksgiving Day. 2. Holidays.] I. Title.

GT4975 .A57 2001
394.2649 – dc21
                              2001000098

Acknowledgments
The author and publishers are grateful to the following for permission to reproduce photographs: Corbis pp. 4, 5 (Ariel Skelley), 13, 19, 27; Gettysburg National Military Park Service pp. 24-25; The Granger Collection pp. 7B, 9, 16, 17, 18, 20-21, 22, 23, 25B, 26; North Wind Pictures pp. 10, 11, 12, 14, 15; Photo Edit p. 28L (A. Ramey), 28R (David Young-Wolff), 29; SuperStock pp. 6-7.

Cover photograph reproduced with permission of Taxi/Getty Images.

Every effort has been made to contact copyright holders of any material reproduced in this book. Any omissions will be rectified in subsequent printings if notice is given to the publisher.

Contents

Some words are shown in bold, **like this**. You can
find out what they mean by looking in the glossary.

Today Is Thanksgiving Day

Winter is coming. In some places, leaves are falling and skies are gray. Yet a happy feeling fills the air. Why? Because today is Thanksgiving Day.

Families have gathered indoors. People are getting ready for a big dinner. Almost every house is filled with the smell of roasting turkey.

Thanksgiving in the Past

Turkey is always popular at Thanksgiving. Long ago, turkey was served only at Thanksgiving. But what does turkey have to do with "giving thanks"?

The answer goes back to a famous party held almost 400 years ago. The hosts were **newcomers** to this land. The guests were Native Americans.

The First Americans

Native Americans came from Asia, thousands of years ago. By 1600 they lived all across what is now North America. Few people from Europe lived here at that time.

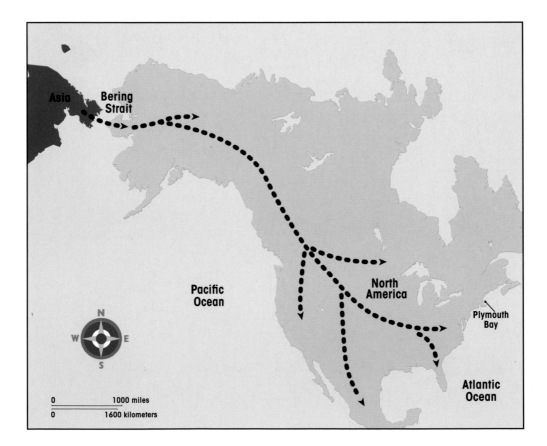

One big Native American tribe was called the
Wampanoag. They had about 30 villages along
the Atlantic **Coast**. Some lived near a place
now known as Plymouth Bay, in Massachusetts.

The Pilgrims Arrive

One day a ship sailed into Plymouth Bay. It was called the *Mayflower*. It carried 102 people from England. They wanted to **settle** in North America.

Many of them were pilgrims. A pilgrim is someone
who travels for religious reasons. The Pilgrims
arrived in North America in November of 1620.

The Puritan Religion

In England these pilgrims had been known as Puritans. They had special ideas about religion. They believed in **simple** living, bible study, and prayer.

But English law said that everyone must belong to the Anglican Church. This rich church was headed by the king. The Puritans would not join the king's church.

This is an Anglican church in Canterbury, England.

A Search for Freedom

Some Puritans were put in jail for not listening to the king. Others decided to leave the country. But they could not find good homes anywhere in Europe.

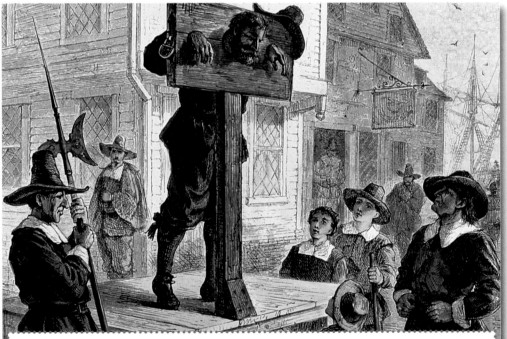

Puritans who did not listen to the king were sometimes punished by having their hands and head locked in a wooden frame.

One group decided to try "the New World"—
North America. These people sailed into
Plymouth Bay in 1620. They arrived two
months after leaving Europe.

Hard Times

The Pilgrims did not know how to get food or **shelter** in the new land. By spring, almost half of them had died. Then some Native Americans came to visit them.

One of these visitors was Massasoit, **chief** of the Wampanoag. Another was Squanto, known then by his Indian name Tisquantum. He lived in Massasoit's village. Tisquantum moved in with the Pilgrims.

A Good Harvest

Tisquantum taught the Pilgrims how to farm and fish in North America. He taught them how to hunt deer and wild turkeys. By fall, the Pilgrims had plenty of food.

English farmers had a **custom**. After a good
harvest, they would have a party. The Pilgrims
decided to have such a party. They invited the
Wampanoag to join them.

The First Thanksgiving

Celebrating a **harvest** was also a Wampanoag **custom**. Their holiday was called the Green Corn **Festival**. **Chief** Massasoit came to the Pilgrim's party with 90 of his people!

One of the main foods at this **feast** was wild turkey. The party lasted for three days. But after it was over, it was mostly forgotten.

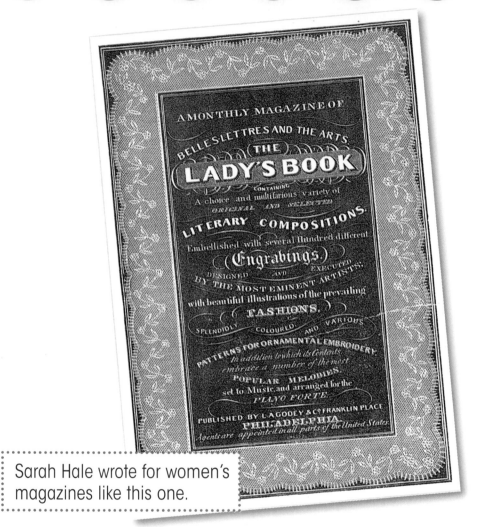

Sarah Hale wrote for women's magazines like this one.

The Thanksgiving Idea

In 1840 a writer named Sarah Hale heard about the Pilgrim's **feast**. She wrote about it for magazines. She said the United States should have a Thanksgiving holiday every year.

Sarah Hale

Hale wrote and spoke about this idea for almost twenty years. At last, President Abraham Lincoln heard what she had to say. Lincoln liked her idea.

A Holiday Is Born

At this time, our country was divided by the **Civil War**. Lincoln thought a Thanksgiving holiday might help bring people together.

Abraham Lincoln

In 1863 Lincoln **declared** a **national** Thanksgiving holiday. He set it for the last Thursday in November. He also made it a yearly holiday.

New Americans

After the **Civil War**, new people came to the United States. Like the Pilgrims, many were seeking freedom. These new Americans gladly celebrated Thanksgiving.

These **newcomers** were used to such a **custom**. Most had **harvest** holidays where they came from. They helped make Thanksgiving one of our most popular holidays.

An American Holiday

Today Americans come from many different places. Few of us are farmers anymore. Yet most of us celebrate Thanksgiving—and in the same way.

We get together with the people we love. We give thanks for the good things we have. Then we sit down together for a great meal.

Important Dates

Thanksgiving Day

1492	Christopher Columbus first explores the Americas
1607	First English people **settle** in North America
1620	Pilgrims arrive at Plymouth Bay, in Massachusetts
1621	The first Thanksgiving takes place
1840	Sarah Hale starts writing about the first Thanksgiving
1863	Abraham Lincoln **declares** Thanksgiving a holiday
1870–1900	More than twelve million people come to the United States from other countries
1941	Fourth Thursday in November named Thanksgiving Day and a **national** holiday by Congress

Glossary

chief   leader

Civil War   American war (1861–1865) between the Northern states and Southern states

coast   land near an ocean or sea

custom   something people always do on special days or for certain events

declare   announce something

feast   party at which much is eaten

festival   time of celebration

harvest   what a farm grows in a season

national   having to do with the whole nation

newcomers   people who have just arrived in a new place

settle   make a home in a new place

shelter   something that covers or protects

simple   not fancy; plain

Find Out More

Erlbach, Arlene and Herbert Erlbach. *Thanksgiving Day Crafts.* Berkeley Heights, NJ: Enslow, 2005.

Kessel, Joyce K. *Squanto and the First Thanksgiving.* Minneapolis, Minn.: Lerner, 2005.

Schuh, Mari C. *Thanksgiving Day.* Mankato, Minn.: Capstone, 2003.

Index